Coloring Book for Adults

Merry Christmas

Christmas Coloring Book for Adults Relaxation

MantraCraft™

This Coloring Book belongs to:

Color Test Page

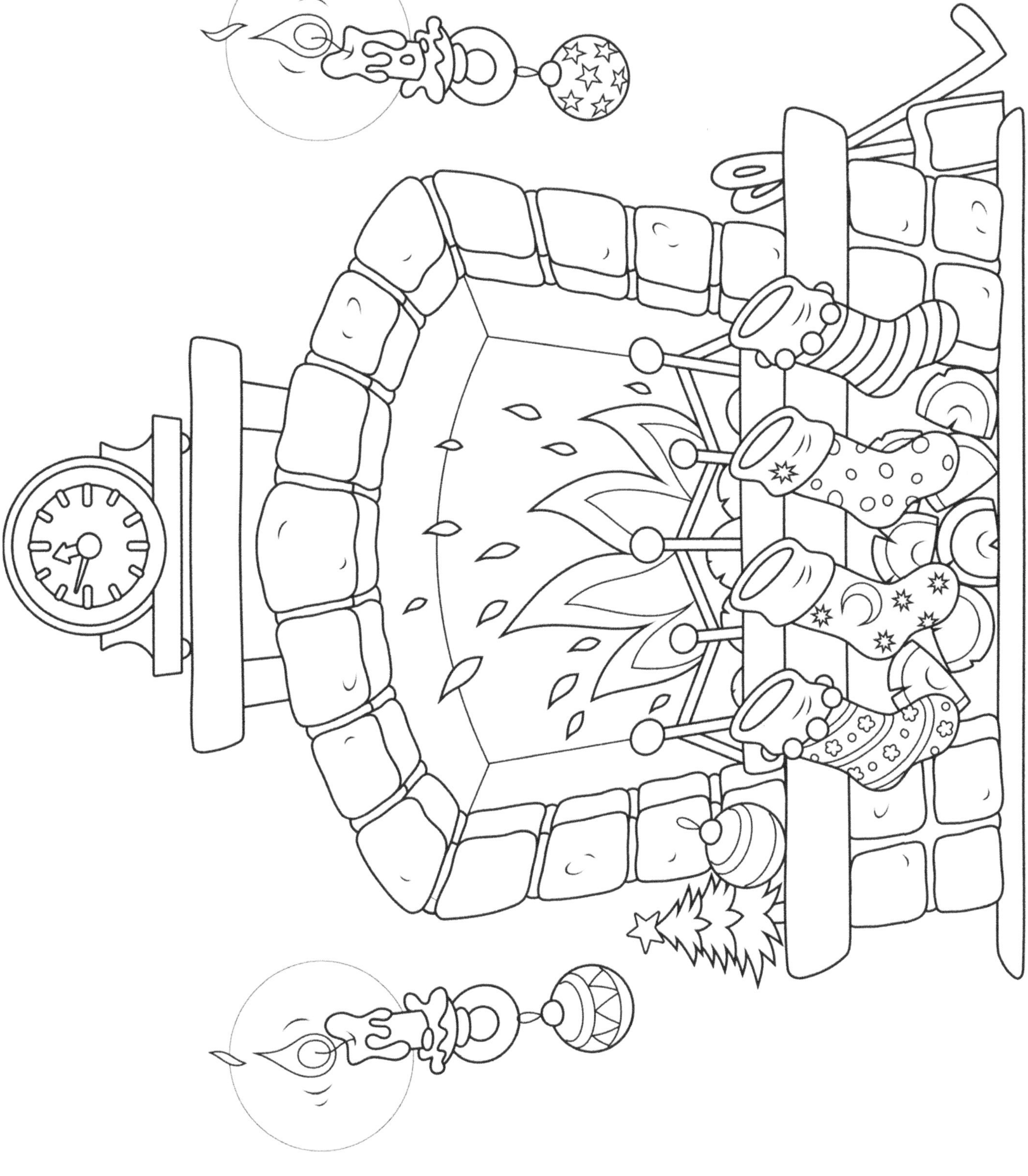

Merry
Christmas

Merry Christmas

MERRY CHRISTMAS

Merry Christmas

Merry
Christmas

Merry
Christmas

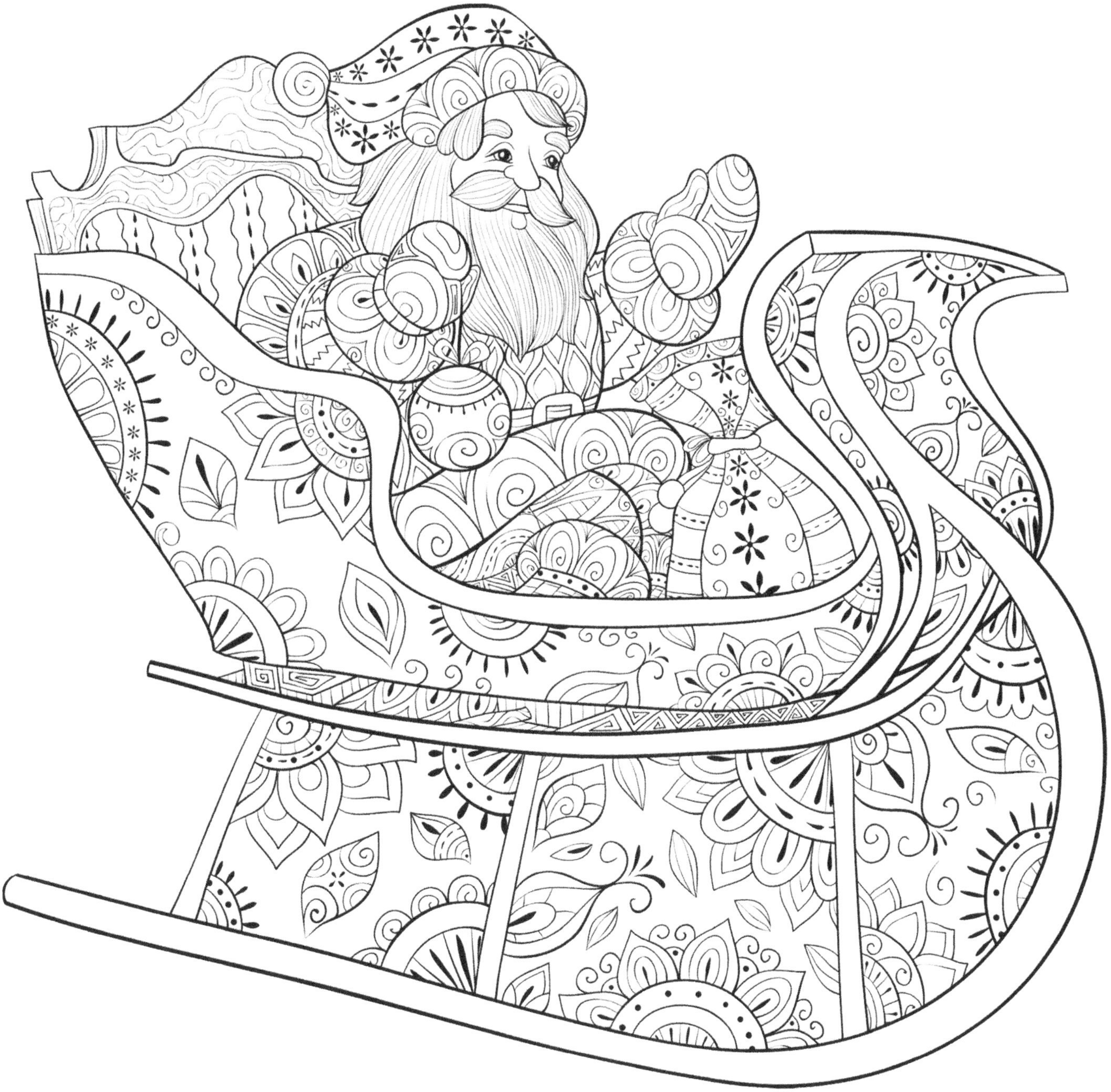

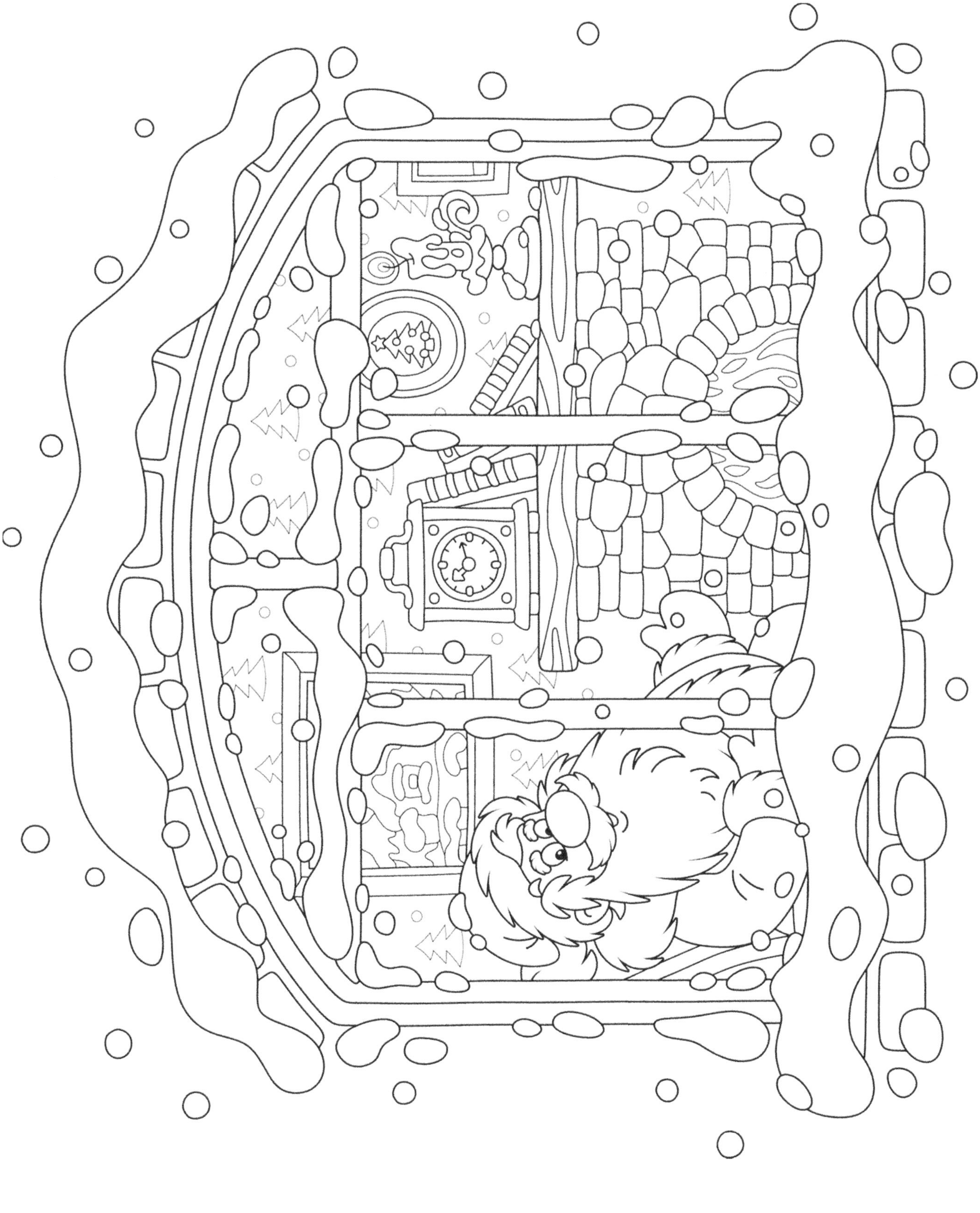

Made in the USA
Monee, IL
20 November 2020

48692441R00063